A Den in the Wood

Explorer Challenge

What lives in
this nest?

OXFORD
UNIVERSITY PRESS

Mum, Biff, Chip and
Kipper went to a wood.
Floppy was sniffing.

Then he ran off.

Chip and Biff ran up to Floppy.

"It is an animal," said Biff.
"Go and get Mum."

"That is a fox cub," said Mum.

6

"It has no mum!" said Biff.

"Can we bring it home with us?" said Kipper.

"No," said Mum. "This den is its home."

8

They all hid.

A big fox went to the den.

"That vixen is its mum,"
said Mum.

The vixen was licking
the cub.

"She is giving him a bath," said Mum.

The vixen went into the
den with the cub.

"We must get home," said Mum.
"*This* cub must get a bath!"

Retell the Story

Look at the pictures and retell the story in your own words.

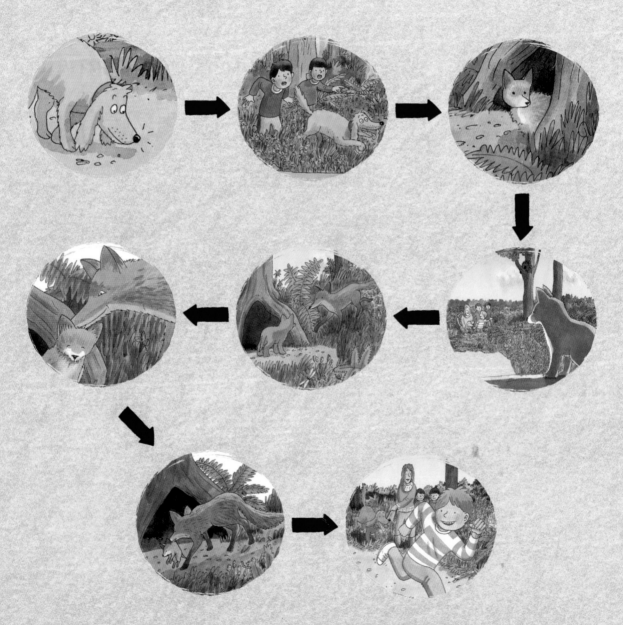

Look Back, Explorers

How did Chip and Biff find the baby fox?

Where did the baby fox live?

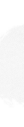

Why did Kipper run off?

Did you find out what lives in this nest?

What's Next, Explorers?

Now read about other animal homes ...

Dens and Nests

Anna Harris
Series created by Roderick Hunt and Alex Brychta

OXFORD

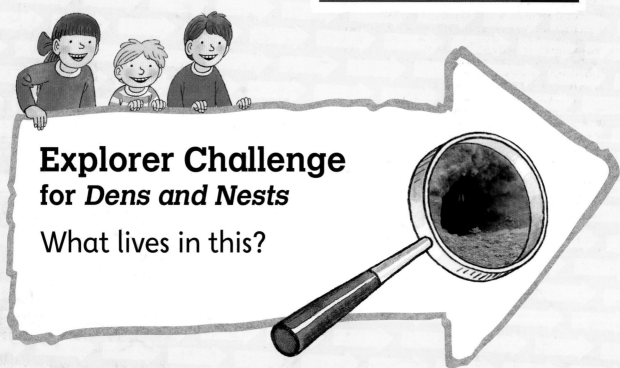

Explorer Challenge
for *Dens and Nests*

What lives in this?